In the Year 2000...

In the Year

2000. . .

Conan O'Brien
and the writers of *Late Night*

RIVERHEAD BOOKS, NEW YORK

Most Riverhead Books are available at special quantity discounts for bulk purchases for sales promotions, premiums, fund-raising or educational use. Special books, or book excerpts, can also be created to fit specific needs.

For details, write: Special Markets, The Berkley Publishing Group, 375 Hudson Street, New York, NY 10014.

Riverhead Books
Published by The Berkley Publishing Group
A division of Penguin Putnam Inc.
375 Hudson Street
New York, New York 10014

First edition: October 1999

The Penguin Putnam Inc. World Wide Web site address is
http://www.penguinputnam.com

Library of Congress Cataloging–in–Publication Data

O'Brien, Conan.
        In the year 2000 / Conan O'Brien and the writers of Late Night.—
1st Riverhead trade pbk. ed.
            p.   cm.
        ISBN 1-57322-771-4
        1. Millennium Humor.   I. Title.
PN6231.M52027   1999
818'.5402—dc21
                                                            99-38811
                                                            CIP

Printed in the United States of America
10 9 8 7 6 5 4 3 2 1

The Writers of *Late Night*

Tom Agna

Chris Albers

Ellie Barancik

Alec Berg

Tommy Blacha

Andrew Blitz

Vernon Chatman

Louis C.K.

Greg Cohen

Janine DiTullio

Jon Glaser

Ned Goldreyer

Amir Gollan

Michael Gordon

Jonathan Groff

Brian Kiley

Marsh McCall

Brian McCann

Bob Odenkirk

Brian Reich

Dave Reynolds

Andy Richter

Jeff Schaffer

Chuck Sklar

Robert Smigel

Brian Stack

Dino Stamatopoulos

Mike Stoyanov

Mike Sweeney

Acknowledgments

Robert Smigel came up with the idea of making ominous predictions for the Year 2000 way back in 1988, and he and I performed the bit that summer in our comedy revue "Happy Happy Good Show." Without Robert, this book would be a tell-all biography about my years as a child star.

My producer, Jeff Ross, gets the show on the air every night and has been a big part of getting this book into your hands. I suspect him of embezzling, but that in no way detracts from his work on this project.

Our head writer, Jonathan Groff, made the lion's share of the creative decisions involved with this book. For his hard work and talent I am rewarding him with a shockingly small cut of the pie.

Our writer's coordinator, Ruth Sinanian, catalogued and compiled our vast supply of predictions and has had to watch several of our writers put pizza down their pants.

La Bamba

For many of our fans, the highlight of the "Year 2000" routine is the eerie, falsetto wail of Richie "La Bamba" Rosenberg. He is living proof that castrating criminals can work.

And, finally, our eternal thanks to Buddha.

Introduction

The future. It fascinates us, frightens us, and fills us with wonder. Throughout history many men have tried to predict what lies ahead, but today their once great "visions" seem sadly off base. Nostradamus claimed man would one day possess a "terrible weapon" capable of destroying the world, Jules Verne thought we'd have "underwater boats," and H. G. Wells promised "great flying machines." Couldn't these great soothsayers have come up with the words "atom bomb," "submarine," and "airplane"? I don't recall ever taking a "great flying machine" to Denver.

Why is the business of predicting the future so difficult? The answer is simple: only God knows our destiny, and Buddha (yes, Buddha … trust me, I'm as shocked as you are) will not reveal his secrets.

Until now. This book is not just another merchandising scheme cooked up by a greedy, General Electric–controlled staff of TV hacks. This is a book of events that will actually take place in the twelve-month span known as the new millennium. Guaranteed. If just one of these prophecies does not come true, we will return your money in full. Simply convert this book to an ion gas with your Molecular De-Stabilizing Rod and inject the cloud into the nearest authorized geotropic tank. A slight burning sensation at the base of your skull will indicate your account has been credited.

And now, let us look to the future. All the way to the Year 2000 …

—Conan O'Brien

In the Year

2000. . .

Man will sometimes write "1999" on his checks.

A race of space aliens with low self-esteem will invade the planet and force us to make them our slaves.

The product "2000 Flushes" will be renamed "A Flush a Year Since Christ Was Born."

In a frank and wide-ranging interview on *Oprah*, the deadly Ebola virus explains that it, too, was just trying to impress Jodie Foster.

In the Year 2000. . .

The Pope will shock the world when he abruptly changes faiths, declaring "I'm a Zeus man now."

Iraq will once again be accused of chemical warfare after spy photos reveal that they've been stockpiling Michael Jordan cologne.

Charles Manson and Son of Sam will be paroled as part of the government's new "Let's Just See What They'll Do" program.

Viagra will no longer come in blue diamonds, but in orange moons, yellow stars, and green clovers.

Crayola Crayons will be forced to change the name of its "Burnt Siena" crayon when Dodgers catcher Carlos Siena spontaneously bursts into flames.

In the Year 2000...

Brooke Shields will marry yet another balding tennis player—Billie Jean King.

Everyone on Earth will become flesh-eating zombies. When the flesh is all gone, they will be dirt-eating zombies. And after that some will reluctantly go to "The Olive Garden."

No longer embarrassed about his religious upbringing, Dr Pepper will begin using his real name, Dr. Sheldon Weintraub.

It will be revealed that the only reason the mitten was invented was because something cute was needed to rhyme with kitten.

Singer Meat Loaf will become the spokesman for a company that makes meat loaf. Vanilla Ice will become a spokesman for a company that makes vanilla ice. And MC Hammer will be arrested for stealing a bike.

Computers will be convinced that it is the year 1900. They will support President McKinley, grow handlebar mustaches, and crack the heads of the filthy Irish.

A teenage boy will smoke his first marijuana cigarette. Within an hour, he will laugh at the thought of a horse riding a jockey, instead of the other way around.

In the Year 2000...

Scientists will discover the secret ingredient in Starbucks Coffee: a chemical that makes people forget they're paying four dollars for a cup of coffee.

The horse and buggy will once again become America's most popular form of transportation, after someone finally realizes that cars don't make poo.

The "Lower" will be declared the official lip of the Winter Olympics.

The lamb shall lie down with the lion. The lion shall lie down with the lamb. And Max Weinberg will try to get in on the action.

A witch is arrested for destroying Michael Bolton's voice. Within hours, the President of the United States grants her a pardon and proclaims that day "National Awesome Witch Day."

Roberto Benigni will lose many of his newfound fans with the release of a sequel to *Life Is Beautiful* called *Life Is Beautiful 2: Electric Boogaloo.*

Kato Kaelin, John Wayne Bobbitt, and Joey Buttafuoco will launch a new theme restaurant … "Planet Dumb-ass."

In the Year 2000...

In a move that leaves legal experts scratching their heads, the Supreme Court will rule that Keanu Reeves is every bit as talented as Sally Jesse Raphael.

Americans are shocked when the Joint Chiefs of Staff admit that sexual harassment is unavoidable in the military because, quote, "All them guns just make us horny."

The Internet will be so overcrowded that most people will make their living strictly through refunds from America Online.

Scuba diving will become the world's most popular sport when the Jacques Cousteau Society announces their discovery that striped bass are easy.

In the Year 2000...

Michael Jackson's fifth son will be born. Like his four brothers before him, his first three words will be "Daddy albino pansy."

Dolphins will no longer perform for our amusement. Except for the ones from Sea World. They'll do as they're told.

An upset Jesus Christ returns to Earth and appears on *The Ricki Lake Show*. The topic: "My Dad Dresses Too Sexy."

Jazz will be replaced by loud slurping noises.

An auto that runs on water will be invented. But it will have a Levi's jeans interior.

A new human emotion named bleem will be recognized. To feel "bleem" is to feel sort of a happy anger.

Policemen will be replaced by robots. The aluminum donut industry will go through the roof.

Jigsaw puzzles will only come in three pieces— but they will be red-hot, and toxic.

In the Year 2000...

Buses for dogs will begin operating in Toronto, Canada. Dogs will complain about bad service.

Toilet paper will be totally computerized at last.

The trend of making teen movies out of classic literature will continue when Dostoyevsky's *Brothers Karamazov* will be remade as *Boner Party USA*.

Corn holders will be outlawed. But there will be more of them than ever.

Black and white Americans will finally be drawn together—by the trial of Bryant Gumbel.

In an attempt to update its image, Disney will produce a hard-core gay porno film. Unfortunately, two of its costars, Chip and Dale, will be tragically suffocated.

Jesus will return to Earth and lead an army of good against the forces of evil. On the cover of *Time* magazine that week: Jewel.

The four-day workweek will become standard, though most employees will be required to work one day each weekend—usually Friday.

In the Year 2000. . .

Crayola Crayons will become so rare that anyone caught coloring outside the lines will be put to death immediately.

Congressmen will be limited to two terms of seven minutes each.

There will be only three chickens left in the world. And they will be very neurotic.

All schools will be replaced by a new building called "The Smarty Maker."

After a horrible accident in India, the *Today* show promotional stunt "Where in the World Is Matt Lauer?" will be changed to "Where in the Tiger's Stool Is Matt Lauer?"

In the Year 2000...

New evidence will prove that Robert Urich
never existed.

Children will be given the right to vote, causing a
landslide victory for President Theodore Mommy.

A new type of dog will be developed—one that can
eat peanut butter with ease.

The term "politically correct" will no longer be
considered politically correct.

Computers will be so small that thousands will fit in a teaspoon. They will be used to perk up the flavor of soup.

Pigeons will be an endangered species. And condors will run amok, blackening the sky.

The hole in the ozone layer will be plugged by technology developed by Sy Sperling.

The government will finally change the word "orange" to a word that's easier to rhyme.

In the Year 2000...

The jack-in-the-box will be replaced by the joe-in-your-face.

Watches will have an hour hand, a minute hand, a second hand, and a real fast hand that doesn't mean nothin'!

Wearing a T-shirt with a drawing of a tuxedo on it will be fresh and funny all over again.

A woman will be President of the United States, and a man will be President of the National Organization for Women.

The color green will be renamed yellowy blue.

Japan will be admitted into the union as the 51st state. The Japanese will be caught completely off guard.

Twentieth Century-Fox will change its name to "Whoa! New Century!" Fox.

Parrots will unionize under the title "Brotherhood of the Repeating Birds." They will strike over and over again.

Bill Clinton will resign from his post—as the Guess Jeans Girl.

In the Year 2000...

When encountering an unpleasant odor, people will no longer say PU. Instead, they will say "WX."

Congress will pass a law making it mandatory for rivers to flow upstream. Rivers will respond with a big "screw you."

The musical term "a-one-and-a-two" will be replaced by "wait, wait, wait—okay, now!"

Aaron Spelling will attempt to enlighten a primitive New Guinea tribe by showing them examples of his work. He will then be eaten.

The faces on Mount Rushmore will get bodies.
Tourists will be horrified by Jefferson's fat ass.

In the Year 2000...

A new kind of Chinese food will satisfy your appetite for *two* hours.

North and South Dakota will merge to form a state called "Oh Man, That's One Big Dakota."

A liver disorder slows the Energizer Bunny measurably. He keeps on going, but complains to anyone who will listen.

1970 will celebrate its thirtieth birthday.
Drunk and alone.

Getting up, walking to the kitchen, and opening a beer will all become Olympic events.

Computers will develop personalities. But John Tesh will stay the same.

The Artist Formerly Known As Prince will not be a symbol but an odor.

The presidential Oath of Office will be drastically shortened. The winning candidate will simply state, "Getta loada me!"

In the Year 2000...

A badly drawn cartoon hamster will be elected to the Senate. He will be indicted on federal racketeering charges, cleared, but still leave office under a cloud of suspicion.

When things go very wrong, it will be a medley of peas and carrots that hit the fan.

A new way to rid our bodies of waste will be called "going number three."

In a truly historic moment, Neil Armstrong's son will land on the moon. His memorable words will be, "This is one small step for man, one giant leap for mankind. And, Dad, I'm gay."

Scientists will revive Einstein's brain, and keep it alive in a jar. It will become a deejay.

In the Year 2000...

Popular campfire songs will include "Kum Bai Ya," "Old MacDonald," and "We Serve Ja-Mar, Our New Alien Master from the Stars."

A 500-page book of inspirational wisdom will ensure world peace for a generation, after falling on and crushing Saddam Hussein.

The Statue of Liberty will be given the spanking of her life, as pages from her book are finally read out loud.

Judicial reforms will allow defendants to enter pleas of "guilty," "not guilty," or "guilty my ass!"

The moon will finally get its sweet revenge—by landing on man!

Canada and America will be united into one country called "Mexico Sucks."

Snow White and the seven dwarfs will undergo a metric conversion to Snow White and the 3.8 dwarfs.

There will be no more professional hockey. But the *Disney on Ice* characters will be allowed to bodycheck.

In the Year 2000...

Kleenex will invent a tissue so soft and lotiony they will have to be wiped up by other tissues.

Romano cheese will be used as currency, making the nickname "stinky pockets" very desirable.

Man's relationship with dogs will forever be altered with the invention of liver-flavored pants.

At long last, a cure for the common cold will be discovered. Unfortunately it will coincide with Ford Motor Company's development of a snot-powered car.

Instead of shaking hands, businesspeople will kiss one another and say, "Thanks for planting one on my pie-hole!"

The Ford Motor Company will be disappointed by consumer reaction to its new subcompact, the Deathbox.

Getting on someone's nerves will no longer be an expression, but a means of mass transportation.

A new improved shower massager from Water Pik is taken off the market after one unit in Michigan is caught trying to "slip it in."

In the Year 2000. . .

A new arm-straightening surgery will be developed to rid us of the unsightly elbow.

The hairbrush will be replaced by a strikingly similar object called the "hairy-goey-where-I-wanty-stick."

Bob Saget will lose yet another acting role, after a casting director proclaims him "too Saget-y."

O. J. Simpson will receive a full presidential pardon. Sadly, it will be from a confused Gerald Ford.

America's belief in angels will be rewarded when thousands are discovered in a secluded valley. They will taste like veal.

In the Year 2000...

Baby seals will no longer be hunted for their fur. They'll be hunted for revenge.

Paris, France, and Paris, Texas, will change places. The Louvre will thereafter be known as "that danged barn with no cows but lotsa fancy pictures."

The earth's atmosphere will be filled by a foul-smelling gas when computers suddenly get tired of "holding it in."

Women's romantic standards will change so radically that an effective pickup line will be "Hey, sugar, I wets the bed."

Mildly retarded space aliens will land in Washington, DC, and demand to be taken to our postmaster general.

Elvis Presley will come forward to reveal he not only faked his death but Redd Foxx's as well.

Genetic engineering will give the average person a life span of over 100 years... and a wingspan of over nine feet.

At the supermarket, customers will be asked the question, "Paper, plastic, or fur?"

In the Year 2000...

Robots will do 80 percent of our housework. But we will do 90 percent of theirs.

Soccer will finally become the most popular sport in America, after its rules are changed to make it more like the show *Home Improvement*.

The lovable Taco Bell dog replaces his famous slogan "Yo quiero Taco Bell" with the more direct slogan "Woo-hoo, diarrhea party USA!"

Women will admit the whole "different from men" thing was a big hoax to get free meals and drinks.

34

Scientists discover that the reason moths are attracted to light is because they need light to be able to read their moth porn.

In the Year 2000...

Confidence in the U.S. dollar will plummet after the motto "In God We Trust" is changed to "I can't believe it's not butter."

Police in rural Wisconsin capture Bigfoot but are forced to release him when he makes bail.

Due to the declining number of champions in the world, Wheaties will change its slogan to "Breakfast of Sexual Deviants."

Air pollution will become so bad that "Who farted?" will be said with a grateful smile.

36

Succumbing to intense public pressure, civic leaders from the Deep South will admit that for years they have been talking funny on purpose.

Tom Hanks will win his eighth Oscar for his starring role in the movie *The Seven-Time Oscar Winner*.

A worldwide rebellion of armed apes on horseback will be crushed by an army of horses on apeback.

The discovery of extraterrestrial life will create a revolution in science, art, and pornography.

In the Year 2000. . .

The polar ice caps will melt, completely flooding the earth, and destroying the set of *Waterworld II*.

Ill-informed aliens will capture two earthlings to breed in captivity: Mel Gibson and RuPaul.

Mexico will rise to world domination, just by knowing when to keep its damn mouth shut.

Christie Brinkley will seek her ninth divorce—from Elizabeth Taylor.

Red ants and black ants will finally stop fighting and get down to some serious lovin'.

Pamela Anderson Lee's breasts will be asked to host the Academy Awards. Only one will accept, leading to the feud of the century.

Man will be able to travel through space at ten times the speed of light after NASA develops a completely useless machine that can slow light way down.

Marine biologists will finally decode the language of the dolphins, only to find they spend most of their time repeating old Cheech and Chong routines.

In the Year 2000. . .

Tired, frustrated, and out of new ideas, hurricanes will finally give up.

Kentucky Fried Chicken will lose market share when it reveals that its new extra, extra, extra crispy recipe is made from human teeth.

A worldwide famine will give rise to the common use of the phrase "Could I have a little more dandruff on that?"

The Miss America Pageant will once again be criticized when the public votes to keep the "faking an orgasm" competition.

The phrase "looking out for number one" will take on a horrific new meaning as the world is overrun by giant, weak-bladdered dogs.

In the Year 2000. . .

In an effort to bring more gays into the military, the U.S. Army will change its slogan from "Be All You Can Be" to "You Go, Girl!"

The new surgeon general will ban the use of the fat substitute Olestra, not because of health concerns, but because he "really digs fat chicks."

Teenagers will really alienate themselves with their latest trend: leprosy.

In an attempt to increase the voters' goodwill, the three branches of government will be renamed Mommy, Daddy, and Grandpa Phil.

The term "coffee, tea, or milk?" will mean "The plane is diving into the sea. I loved you. Oh, I loved you so."

Forks and knives will settle their long-standing feud, when it is discovered that they are both viciously antispatula.

All over the world, McDonald's restaurants will be sprouting up at a rate of ten per day... all by themselves.

With every other conceivable name having been exhausted, all hurricanes will be called simply "that filthy wet son of a bitch."

In the Year 2000...

Switzerland will no longer be neutral after its
scientists develop a nuclear cheese.

Time travel will be so commonplace that Domino's
will change its guarantee to "30 minutes ago or
it's free."

In a rare exception to the First Amendment, the
Supreme Court forbids anyone in the cast of *Friends*
from ever again saying "We're friends offscreen, too."

Sick and tired of communicating via sign language,
Koko the gorilla speaks her very first words—"Me
love you long time, Joe."

Men will finally discover that the reason women go to the bathroom in pairs... is to make out.

In the Year 2000...

The world food shortage will be so severe that midgets will be known as "appetizers."

A miracle drug is discovered that can give a man a continuous rock-hard erection for 30 years. On the downside, it devastates the towel-rack industry.

Cross-dressing will be so humdrum and common-place that talk-show hosts will no longer get a kick out of secretly wearing women's lingerie on the air.

Only two days away from finally eliminating the federal budget deficit, Congress blows it all on one night with a 250-foot-tall hooker.

The radio signals scientists have been sending into outer space will finally get a reply. Their simple message: "Less talk, more rock."

In a controversial move, Ted Kennedy's head will be added to Mount Rushmore. Not a sculpture—his actual head.

In an effort to revive his flagging career, actor Dom DeLuise will change his name to Dom de Dom Dom.

Every product sold in America's grocery stores will be lemon-scented, except lemons.

In the Year 2000...

Faxes will give way to a new and more horrific form of instantaneous communication—The Screaming Toilet.

Violent crime will become so rampant that New York's street signs will say "stab" and "don't stab."

Packaged Toll House cookies will become so moist and chewy that people will no longer fear death.

Hooters will open a restaurant featuring its original waitresses. It will be called Saggers.

All magazines will go out of business when it's discovered that there is absolutely nothing more to learn about the cast of *Friends*.

Plants the world over will stop producing oxygen in an attempt to rid the earth of "the Michael Bolton Problem."

The environmental movement will lose so much support that KFC will stand for "Kentucky Fried Condors."

Medical research will become so amazingly advanced that the Ebola virus will be used as a crunchy dessert topping.

In the Year 2000. . .

Rush Limbaugh will rethink his conservative views after he discovers a welfare mother and her three children living in the folds of his neck.

The term "March Madness" will take on a whole new meaning when March arrives, wearing a dress, claiming to be April.

In the worst hospital mix-up ever, doctors in Florida will accidentally amputate a man's leg, hollow it out, and play it like a flute.

Babies all around the world will become bored with the taste of breast milk, and will insist on a new Kool-aid drink: Captain Nippleberry.

In an effort to outdo her previous halftime shows at the Super Bowl, Diana Ross will exit the stadium and ascend to the right hand of God, where she will judge the living and the dead.

In the Year 2000. . .

Engineers will design a fast, efficient automobile powered solely by the driver's hatred for Kathie Lee Gifford.

Steve Forbes will spend his last 40 dollars in a desperate attempt to become a Harlem Globetrotter.

The entertainment world will be shocked to learn that more than half the characters in the beloved Peanuts comic strip are flamboyant homosexuals.

Lay's potato chips will be forced to change their slogan from "You can't eat just one" to "Sorry about all the dead fat people."

An entomologist will discover a new social structure among honeybees—there are queens, workers, drones, and pollen whores.

Children will begin growing up so fast that the nursery rhyme "One, Two, Buckle My Shoe" will be replaced by the more realistic "One, Two, Dammit, I'm Pregnant."

Dr. Jack Kevorkian will die and go to heaven. The next day, seven angels will be found dead in the back of God's van.

As a result of his abduction and disappearance, John Tesh will be known as the Missing, Missing Link.

In the Year 2000...

Magician David Copperfield will finally reveal how he does his amazing tricks: he's Jesus.

The world is stunned to finally learn the identity of the real father of Michael Jackson's child: Richard Simmons.

Self-adhesive stamps will prove so popular that the post office will introduce their logical successor—stamps that lick you back.

Scientists will improve the quality of life when they isolate the gene that causes people to sign up for the Columbia Record and Tape Club.

A two-month-old infant will sue himself for sexual harassment immediately after he catches himself sucking his own thumb.

Ross Perot is finally elected president. Analysts attribute his victory to voters' dissatisfaction with Washington politics, and their great fear of his giant robot.

Krazy Glue will be replaced by a far more powerful adhesive: "Psychotic Ax-Murderer Glue."

After two terms as vice president and a grueling campaign, Al Gore will finally be elected to the office he's been seeking his whole life: "America's Favorite Honky."

In the Year 2000. . .

Mike Tyson's record will drop to 40 wins and 500 losses, after opponents realize he's extremely vulnerable to the "your shoelaces are untied" trick.

Dr. Kevorkian will announce his retirement after reducing the world population to himself and Cindy Crawford.

A daring and controversial plan to capture Bigfoot will fail when he sends a friend to accept his Oscar for him.

Condoms will be so well formed and comfortable that most men will prefer dating *them*.

Women will no longer be required to wear tops in public. But men will.

In the Year 2000. . .

Scientists will be shocked to discover that the monkey responsible for the Ebola virus was also responsible for the Macarena.

The shocking autopsy of Sandra Day O'Connor will reveal that Ruth Bader Ginsburg was the first woman to serve on the Supreme Court.

Synchronized swimming will become the highest-rated event in the Australian Olympics when its name is changed to "wet babes all doing the same thing."

Arabs and Jews will suddenly stop being enemies after an adorable six-year-old blond boy points out that they both enjoy many of the same foods.

Vegetarianism will fall out of fashion overnight when plants everywhere suddenly figure out how to scream.

America's future will be jeopardized by the latest trend among teenagers: Spay-and-Neuter parties.

Automobiles will no longer be equipped with mandatory air bags, because people will be equipped with mandatory breast implants.

In the Year 2000...

After thousands of years of joy and togetherness, the long honeymoon between flies and horse manure will finally end.

Concerned that she has nothing left to expose to filmgoers and worried about her flagging career, Demi Moore spontaneously develops a third breast.

During closing ceremonies at Wimbledon, an aging Queen Elizabeth will declare herself champion. She'll then yell to the crowd, "Hey! Peasants! Watch me fly!" and leap 30 feet to her death.

The family airplane will replace the family car. Teenagers will be forced to have their first sexual experiences in the baggage compartment.

The language of the cow is finally deciphered. The word "moo" means "I dare you to slaughter and eat me."

America rejoices as General Colin Powell finally agrees to accept the job as the nation's 43rd Batman.

The Mafia will completely run out of animal nicknames, after the death of Jimmy "The Duckbilled Platypus" Santoli.

In the Year 2000...

Vegetarians will be horrified to learn that plants do have thoughts and feelings. The main thing they think and feel: that vegetarians are incredibly annoying.

Starbucks makes franchise history by opening a Starbucks inside an existing Starbucks.

President Pat Buchanan will build a chain-link electrified fence around America and refuse to give Mexicans back their Wiffle balls.

After millions of years of stability, the food chain will suddenly reverse. Zebras will hunt down lions. Pop-Tarts will hunt down man.

In the Year 2000...

Hootie and the Blowfish break up over creative differences, and reform as Hootie and Garfunkel.

The birds and the bees will finally get it on, creating the most feared creature of all time: the bumblehawk.

The public panics when subway gunman Bernard Goetz and Jack Kevorkian join forces and start shooting people who look sick.

Johnson's will replace its "no more tears" baby shampoo with the much more useful "no more poo that looks like mustard" baby shampoo.

64

The military changes its "don't ask, don't tell" policy in favor of the controversial "prove you're gay, I'll be waiting in the foxhole" policy.

After retiring from the White House, President Clinton requests and is granted an appointment to a newly formed position in the Department of Health. His title? National Breast and Fried Food Inspector.

Boutros Boutros-Ghali will suffer yet another humiliation when the world decides his name is too ridiculous and forces him to answer to "Johnny Bacon-Bits."

In the Year 2000. . .

After a three-year debate, Congress finally hammers out a compromise on Social Security reform: benefits will remain the same, but the name "Social Security" will be changed to "Here's Your Check, You Money-grubbing Old Crone."

Archaeologists in the Sinai Desert will discover the long-lost 11th Commandment: thou shalt not sweat it if that adultery one cramps your style.

Bob Dole celebrates his 77th birthday in the Oval Office. Security guards discover him, though, and drag him kicking and screaming back to his tour group.

In an effort to be even more politically correct, school textbooks will no longer refer to George Washington as our first president, but as a mentally challenged Asian-American in a wheelchair.

People all over the world are shocked and angry to learn that the billions of dollars they have donated have gone to fighting the astrological sign Cancer.

Jails will become so overcrowded that prisoners will be forced to sodomize one another, as a space saving measure.

In the Year 2000...

Aunt Jemima and Mrs. Butterworth will damage their wholesome family image when they admit that they frequently taste each other's syrup.

An impoverished O. J. Simpson announces that he's coming out of retirement, and will begin murdering people immediately.

Bob Barker will again rise to national prominence, this time for his campaign to spay and neuter the Kennedys.

Organ transplants will be so safe and easy that hard-core alcoholics will be able to rent a liver for big weekends.

Birds will become so lazy that they will no longer fly, but instead will lounge by the side of the road and toss their droppings at passing cars.

In the Year 2000. . .

Nursing homes will phase out the song "Happy Birthday," and replace it with a new song entitled "What's the Point, Blue-Hair?"

College tuition becomes so expensive that only one person in America can afford it. But he parties too much and flunks out.

As more and more people start having sex with robots, it will become increasingly embarrassing to buy a can of WD-40.

McDonald's is forced to close its restaurant on Mars because of the high costs of shipping acne to its workers there.

People will live in large, underwater cities. Fourth of July fireworks displays will be replaced by large-scale synchronized flushing.

In the most unwelcome medical breakthrough ever, a cure is finally found for obesity: nudism.

China will angrily give Hong Kong back to the British, saying, "Here, you get the smell out."

ABC newsman Sam Donaldson will be so old that his toupee will start wearing a toupee.

In the Year 2000...

It will be discovered that leprechauns are, in fact, real, but not, in fact, Irish.

There will be one tenth as many homeless people roaming the streets of America. Unfortunately, each homeless person will be ten times his original size.

Virtual pets will clear the last hurdle in replacing real pets when Chinese restaurants start putting them in their food.

Eighty-year-old women will be able to give birth, using a revolutionary new medical technique that keeps 20-year-olds in labor for over 60 years.

President Clinton himself will propose a compromise in the ongoing Paula Jones case. The President will admit that he propositioned Jones in 1991, if she will admit that he's, quote, "hung like a Clydesdale."

In his even more shocking rematch with Evander Holyfield, Mike Tyson will finish the fight a full five pounds heavier than when he started.

Coke and Pepsi will merge and form a company so powerful and arrogant that they will successfully market a soft drink called "Drink this crap, you ugly loser-face."

In the Year 2000...

Jesus Christ returns to Earth but quickly leaves when he discovers the 55-cent Egg McMuffin deal has expired.

Dogs will finally realize that people are watching them when they sniff each other's butts and will begin charging admission.

Life on Mars is finally discovered when *Pathfinder II* stops momentarily to analyze some soil and is immediately surrounded by guys with squeegees.

The original Ten Commandments will be found in the Sinai Desert. The little heart drawn over every letter "i" will lead scholars to believe that God is a 12-year-old girl.

In the Year 2000. . .

Jimmy Carter will once again run for president, this time as the nominee of the "Where's the Harm in Humoring the Old Fool?" party.

Endangered animals will make such a dramatic comeback that every American back porch will be equipped with a bald-eagle zapper.

To combat drug use, the government breeds a marijuana-eating locust but abandons the project when the locust won't stop talking about Pink Floyd.

The American educational system will be thrown into chaos when a grown man in Illinois actually uses algebra in everyday life.

A retired President Clinton will write his memoirs, and will be sued for plagiarism by Wilt Chamberlain.

The drinking age is lowered to three in order to "keep the bastards quiet."

To simplify police work, a new federal law will require all known sex offenders to change their name to Kennedy.

In the Year 2000...

The U.S. will stop printing money, and people will be forced to barter. A goat will get you a case of beer and a Michael Bolton album will get you a vicious beating.

Outlaw Jesse James will return from the grave to avenge his death. Unfortunately, because he was cremated, he won't be able to do much more than throw himself in people's eyes and make them tear up real bad.

The Mir space station will finally crash to Earth, but not before completing its most important experiment: to see how long it takes for a big hunk of Russian-made crap to fall out of the sky.

Mormons will decide that their religion is too strict and begin drinking coffee, the occasional beer, and the blood of the elderly.

The public demands that the NBA expand to a 52-week schedule. Not for the love of the game, but to keep Shaquille O'Neal too busy to make movies.

Space aliens will come to Earth intending to deliver a message of universal peace and wisdom. Unfortunately, they land on the stage at *Def Comedy Jam* and end up telling jokes about how big their women's booties are.

In the Year 2000...

China's overpopulation problem will reach horrifying new levels when people discover what an exceptionally pleasurable lubricant duck sauce is.

Scientists will discover the reason for the Loch Ness monster's seclusion: it doesn't like Scottish people.

The world is rocked when Colonel Sanders's secret recipe is discovered to be one part salt, one part sage, and the gayest chicken money can buy.

After too many years of nonstop rampages, El Niño decides to check himself into the Betty Ford Clinic. Three months later he emerges as the 11th husband of Elizabeth Taylor.

Volvo introduces its safest automobile yet.
Upon impact, Anna Nicole Smith gets up from
underneath the dashboard, pushes her breasts
into your face and squeals "I love you, Daddy!"

In the Year 2000...

Man will devolve back into apes while apes will evolve into man. Women will not be affected.

A bitter Richard Gere will turn his back on Buddhism, after his former friend the Dalai Lama beats him out for the lead in *American Gigolo 2*.

The planets Jupiter, Mars, and Neptune will suddenly stop spinning when they realize they can get just as strong a head rush sniffing glue.

God will schedule a press conference to announce the firing of Jesus and the hiring of Jets coach Bill Parcells.

After a combined 134 years in broadcasting, Mike Wallace, Morley Safer, and Andy Rooney will finally leave *60 Minutes* to join the Rolling Stones.

Zoologists will finally figure out why pandas in captivity refuse to mate: they're holding out for a three-way.

America realizes that Jenny McCarthy is more than a big-breasted blonde with goofy facial expressions and finally begins to appreciate her dynamite ass.

An even more shocking home videotape of Pamela and Tommy Lee will come out, this one featuring the two of them adding and subtracting.

In the Year 2000. . .

God at last reveals Himself to humans, who are shocked and appalled by His really bad comb-over.

In an effort to make fast food even faster, McDonald's will begin pumping their food directly into customers' stomachs. To keep pace, Burger King will pump their food directly into people's toilets.

The Spice Girls will once again be famous when MTV's *The Real World* decides to focus on five middle-aged, out-of-work hags.

The hyphen will be replaced by the dash and the dash will be replaced by the hyphen. No one will notice.

Jerry Springer will make a desperate attempt at respectability when he cancels *Big-Breasted Nympho Cheerleaders* and replaces it with *Big-Breasted Nympho Economists*.

In an alarming press conference, Dom DeLuise will finally reveal that even he can no longer tell the difference between himself and Paul Prudhomme.

An elderly President Clinton will become so stooped and bent over that no one will be able to tell him apart from his penis.

John Glenn's record as the oldest man in space will be broken when an exploding amplifier sends Keith Richards hurtling into the stratosphere.

In the Year 2000...

An experiment to test the effect of secondhand marijuana smoke on blind people will end in slaughter, when their Seeing Eye dogs get the munchies.

Shocking new evidence reveals that on that fateful day in 1991, then-Governor Clinton actually summoned a person named "Paul A. Jones" to his hotel room to show off his "big clock."

The terms "hillbilly" and "cracker" will be considered as offensive as any other racial slur. The term "white trash," however, will still be completely acceptable, and will continue to bring joy to millions.

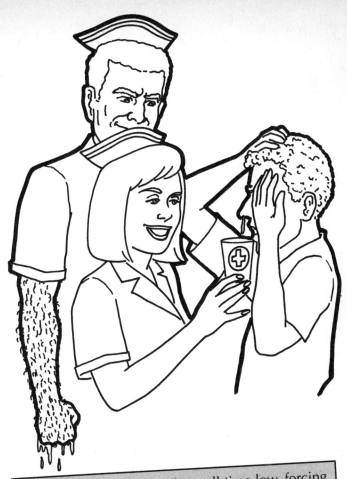

Blood-bank supplies reach an all-time low, forcing the Red Cross to randomly punch people in the face and hold a cup under their nose.

In the Year 2000. . .

After 28 years together, Hall and Oates split up, forming two separate bands: "Hall" and "Oates." Ironically, Oates will be in "Hall" and Hall will be in "Oates."

A real live angel will be born in Louisiana. Unfortunately, his parents will sell him to the carnival, where he will be billed as "Ringhead, the Hideous Birdboy."

Oprah Winfrey will again take on the Texas cattle industry, this time defeating 40 of their biggest steers in an exciting monthlong "graze-off."

The Postman, Part 2 will be released. It will be a moving, award-winning documentary about Kevin Costner's current job as a low-paid guy who sorts mail.

Jesus will return to Earth, supposedly to help us begin a new era of peace and spiritual awakening. In reality, however, he'll spend most of his time golfing with Vernon Jordan.

An aging and senile ex-President Clinton will legally change his name to "Bubba Wanna Burger Chief Booty Knocker."

A desperate, sex-starved Monica Lewinsky will be spotted licking rocks at the base of Mount Rushmore.

In the Year 2000...

All dogs will be issued photo IDs, finally sparing them the humiliation of sniffing each other's butts.

The two sheep cloned in 1997 will be exposed as frauds when their costumes are unzipped to reveal an apologetic Milli Vanilli.

Major League Baseball will finally reach the limits of expansion with the addition of its latest franchise: "The Jeff Higgins of 143 Mercer Street, Hartsdale, New York, Blue Socks."

Bill Gates will go from a billionaire to a trillionaire, then blow it all on three-card monte.

In a shameless attempt to get free stuff, an unnamed talent at NBC will begin mentioning company names in his book. He'll name companies like Guinness, Ferrari, and Trojan.

Tired of feeling exploited, a furious *Titanic* raises itself from the ocean floor proclaiming, "I may be rusty and old, but I'm hung like a horse, so give me a piece of that money pie."

Rain forest destruction will no longer be a concern, when scientists discover that the rain forest is a drunken, no-good son of a bitch.

In the Year 2000...

Penguins will begin having senior proms but will surprisingly *still* rent tuxes.

Thousands of men will successfully climb Mount Everest after Madonna legally changes her name to Mount Everest.

A remorseful O. J. Simpson will make a shocking confession: he often rented from Avis.

Pigs will convert to Orthodox Judaism but, shockingly, will start eating pork.

Time travel will become a reality, allowing Michael Jackson to travel back to 1965 and "take a nap" with himself.

In the Year 2000...

Computers will finally be able to simulate human feelings. Unfortunately, the only one they choose to act on is "horny."

Mothers will no longer call for "time-outs" when disciplining their children, but instead will use the more accurate phrase "Now go sit in the corner and shut your pie-hole while Mommy has a drink."

Christians worldwide will be delighted when DNA tests prove once and for all that the image on the Shroud of Turin is, in fact, Ted Nugent.

As a conclusive sign that society has grown more violent, the "give a penny, take a penny" dish at the cash registers will be replaced with the far less popular "give a penny, take a beating" dish.

A penniless Monica Lewinsky will be unable to pay her hefty legal fees. When asked to comment, her lawyers say, "Don't worry, we've made other arrangements."

Women begin eating fried foods and smoking cigarettes more than ever. Experts attribute this to the popularity of the new fashion magazine *Fat Ass, Bad Breath Vogue.*

In the Year 2000...

Scientists will dissect the body of Kathie Lee Gifford. Despite her horrific screams.

India finally agrees to stop further nuclear testing after it realizes that it already has an unlimited supply of the world's most explosive substance: Indian food.

Hypochondriacs the world over will finally stop believing that they're sick all the time. When they all die of disease.

Researchers prove that life does in fact imitate art. Unfortunately, the art it imitates is the movie *Tango and Cash*.

The United States Armed Forces will be composed entirely of robots. Surprisingly, this will not end the problem of gays in the military.

In the Year 2000. . .

Authorities discover a foolproof means of identifying the clinically insane: tracking order forms for the new George and Barbara Bush sex video.

The old adage that "Guns don't kill people, people kill people" is forever deemed invalid when a woman gives birth to a gun, and it grows up and stabs her.

The Catholic Church will decide that it needs a leader one step above the Pope. His title will be "Captain Pope-tastic."

Rock music will all be done by computers, and as a result, computers will get a lot more oral sex.

Incredibly, a priest, a rabbi, and a Buddhist monk will actually find themselves on a crashing plane that has only one parachute. Ironically, that parachute will have been packed by a Polish guy, and will contain only camping equipment.

Microsoft will go out of business and Bill Gates will be bankrupt after the disastrous release of their latest product: Windows Kevin Costner.

A dolphin trainer at Sea World will shock the audience by getting down on one knee and asking his dolphin to marry him. The dolphin will say no, not because the man is human, but because he's not Jewish.

In the Year 2000. . .

Thanks to new telephone technology, call waiting will no longer involve hearing a little click, but rather, feeling a little tongue.

Pornography finally gets accepted into the mainstream, when the Academy Award for Best Actor goes to Long Dong Hanks.

A shocking exposé in the *New York Times* reveals that the Supreme Court is nothing more than regular court with sour cream and tomatoes.

Viagra will become a popular doggie snack; as a result, dachshunds will become nine feet long and rock hard.

Sales of "I Can't Believe It's Not Butter" will decline rapidly when its name is inexplicably changed to "I Can't Believe It's Not Hitler."

Tired of all the infidelity, Hillary Clinton will divorce President Clinton and remarry, becoming Mrs. Charlie Sheen.

Plants will stop relying on sunlight, soil, and water when they taste their first chili dog.

The letter "G" decides it's had enough, and forces Kenny G to change his name to Kenny H.

In the Year 2000...

Conan O'Brien's book about his own sexual escapades will be banned by school boards—not for explicit descriptions of sex, but for inaccurate descriptions of sex.

Boomerangs will no longer come back immediately after you throw them but rather when they're damn good and ready.

Mark McGwire will hit 80 home runs, but will alienate his many fans when he declares on national TV: "I am so impressed with what I've done I could just do myself in the butt."

After several cohosts of *The View* disappear mysteriously, new cohosts are warned not to accept Star Jones's traditional welcoming gift: a sleeping bag made of French bread.

In the Year 2000...

Willard Scott will be tried for mass murder, when studies show that almost everyone he wishes "Happy 100th Birthday" to dies mysteriously within ten years.

A 4000-year-old man will be found in the Alps—alive. His first words to his rescuer: "Wait a second. You're a guy, and you're wearing an earring?"

Calista Flockhart will attempt to prove she's not anorexic by eating Kate Moss.

Flags across the nation will fly at half-mast, in honor of America's new holiday, Half-Mast Day.

The Beastie Boys will finally become Beastie Men, when they go through Beastie Puberty.

Peace will finally come to the Middle East when Israeli Prime Minister Ehud Barak falls in love with and marries Yasir Arafat's beard.

The west wind will no longer be called a zephyr but rather "the wind formerly known as a zephyr." The east wind will still be called "Meat Loaf."

A scientist will win the Nobel Prize when he miraculously transplants actual soul from Aretha Franklin to Mariah Carey.

In the Year 2000. . .

The 62nd Annual Academy Awards will run so long there won't be any time left for the 63rd Annual Academy Awards.

The statement "If guns are outlawed, only outlaws will have guns" will be outlawed.

Baldness will finally be cured; upon hearing the news, Burt Reynolds will set free his 400 woodchucks.

The Pillsbury Doughboy gets playfully poked in the stomach, giggles, and then blurts out to a shocked America that he has a drinking problem.

Scandal rocks the world of rap music when Sir-Mix-A-Lot admits that he lied, and actually does *not* like big butts.

Hollywood super-agent Mike Ovitz further secures his reputation as the best negotiator of all time when he lands a huge three-picture deal for his newest client: diarrhea.

The name Kathie Lee will be the single most popular name in America. When people start naming their asses.

Switzerland will finally stop being completely neutral when it admits that compared to early Aerosmith albums, the new ones suck.

In the Year 2000. . .

Air pollution will make people so stupid that Pia Zadora will get famous all over again.

Bill Gates will be impoverished after spending all of his 70 billion dollars on research to fight dorkiness.

The African-American supermodel Roshumba will find new competition from an Orthodox Jewish supermodel, Rosh Shushomba.

Historical revisionists will shock the world with the revelation that Fuzzy Wuzzy was not a bear who had no hair, but instead was a cruel dictator who murdered his own people.

In an official policy change, Mob hit men will no longer give their victims the "Kiss of Death," but the far more pleasurable "Hummer of Doom."

In the Year 2000...

Mark McGwire will become the richest man on Earth when he finally learns to tie a string to every ball he hits.

Ballpark Franks will no longer "plump when you cook 'em." Instead, they will spit at you and call you a whore.

Elizabeth Dole will be elected president, making Bob Dole America's "First Man," something already verified by fossil records.

The first openly gay hurricane, Richard, will emerge from the Atlantic and firmly but gently punish the tip of Florida.

The human appendix will solidify its reputation for being useless, when it is caught behind the liver watching game shows and smoking pot.

Former Vice-President Dan Quayle is rushed to the hospital after talking an intern into putting a cigar in his penis.

The moon hitting your eye like a big pizza pie will no longer be "amore," but a defense for a justifiable homicide.

Secret documents will reveal why Baskin-Robbins stopped at 31 flavors. Flavor 32 tasted too much like Gary Coleman.

In the Year 2000. . .

Two billionaire balloonists successfully circumnavigate the globe, setting a new record. Not for distance, but for number of people who don't care.

Monica Lewinsky's famous blue dress will be sold at auction to an evil industrialist, who will use the DNA to clone his own army of horny, lying rednecks.

Soon after the country's most beloved TV personality is killed in a skydiving accident, industrious fans turn tragedy into opportunity by opening Oprah Crater Park.

An angry and embarrassed ozone layer will slap American scientists with a 20-million-dollar libel suit for, quote, "the demeaning and degrading discussion regarding the size of my hole."

The number "3" will be outlawed, thereby making all omelettes either too large or too small.

The film *The Matrix II* is released, containing the most amazing special effects to date, including an unbelievable scene where it appears Keanu Reeves can read.

In the Year 2000...

Dolphins will be able to speak. But they will be boring and their breath will stink.

Charles Manson is finally released from prison when the parole board cannot satisfactorily answer his question, "What makes me any worse than Joan Lunden?"

At the stroke of midnight in the new millennium, actor Ben Affleck will grab the microphone from Dick Clark, look into the camera, and say, "Wake up, America, I'm a dope."

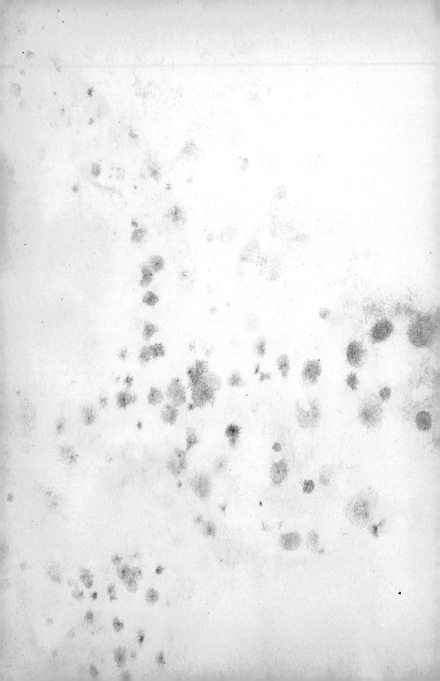